Contents

Glossary words

When a word is printed in **bold**, you can look up its meaning in the Glossary on page 31.

The sport

Triathlon is an **endurance** sport and is a great way to keep fit and to maintain a healthy lifestyle. Triathlon racing is a serious sport performed by **elite** athletes. It is also a fun pastime enjoyed by people of all ages and abilities. Triathlon combines the sports of swimming, cycling and running.

Triathlons are a popular way of getting fit.

Did you know?

Members of the San Diego Track Club in the United States of America came up with the idea of triathlon racing in the early 1970s.

The history of triathlon

Triathlon racing developed as an alternative form of training for runners and cyclists who were bored with their normal training programs. The idea of the triathlon became so popular that triathlon racing soon became a sport of its own. The first triathlon was held in 1978 on the island of Hawaii and was named the 'Hawaiian Ironman Race'. In the 1980s, after the success of this event, shorter triathlons were introduced in Australia and the United States of America. Since then, the popularity of triathlon racing has grown dramatically. Triathlon events are now held in countries all over the world, including most of Europe and Canada.

Getting into Triathlon

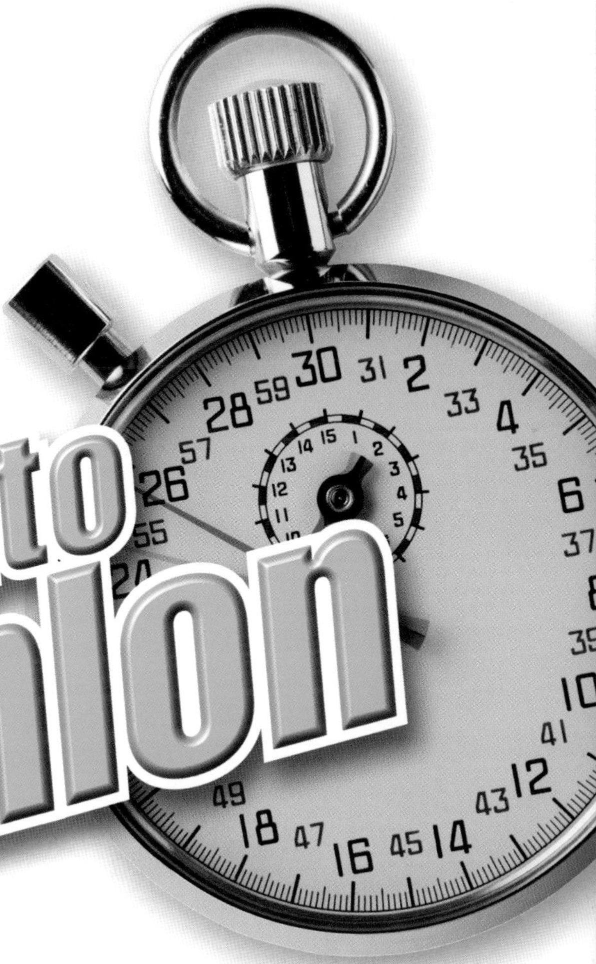

Luke Davis and Damien Davis

First published in 2006 by
MACMILLAN EDUCATION AUSTRALIA PTY LTD
627 Chapel Street, South Yarra 3141

Visit our website at www.macmillan.com.au

Associated companies and representatives throughout the world.

National Library of Australia
Cataloguing-in-Publication data

Davis, Luke, 1983–.
Triathlon.

Includes index.
For middle to upper primary school aged children.
ISBN 978 0 7329 9990 2.
ISBN 0 7329 9990 1.

1. Triathlon – Juvenile literature. I. Davis, Damien. II. Title. (Series: Getting into (South Yarra, Vic.)).

796.4257

Edited by Helena Newton
Text and cover design by Cristina Neri, Canary Graphic Design
Illustrations by Nives Porcellato and Andy Craig
Photo research by Legend Images

Printed in China

Acknowledgements
The author and the publisher are grateful to the following for permission to reproduce copyright material:

Front cover image, Emma Carney finishes swim leg of triathlon, courtesy of Newspix; inset image of stopwatch courtesy of Photodisc.

Australian Sports Commission, pp. 5, 8, 13, 21, 22, 23, 24, 26, 28; Thomas Coex/AFP/Getty Images, pp 20, 30; Pierre-Philippe Marcou/AFP/Getty Images, p. 29; Brian Bahr/ALLSPORT/Getty Images, p. 12; Marco Garcia/Getty Images, p. 7; Nigel Marple/ Getty Images, p. 19; Adam Pretty/Getty Images, p. 6 (right); David Stluka/Getty Images, p. 9; Jonathan Wood/Getty Images, pp. 4, 6 (left), 11; Photodisc, p. 1; Photolibrary/Age Foto, p. 25; Photolibrary/Veer/Haddon, p. 27.

While every care has been taken to trace and acknowledge copyright, the publisher tenders their apologies for any accidental infringement where copyright has proved untraceable. Where the attempt has been unsuccessful, the publisher welcomes information that would redress the situation.

Disclaimer
The activities described in this book are potentially dangerous, and could result in serious injury if attempted by inexperienced persons. The authors and publisher wish to advise readers that they take no responsibility for any mishaps that may occur as a result of persons attempting to perform the activities described in this book.

Going the distance

A triathlon race is a challenging event for fit people of all ages. A triathlon is made up of three legs, or sections. Each leg of a triathlon is like a race in itself, and when all three are put together it becomes a long and tiring event. The first leg of a triathlon is the swim. After completing the swimming leg, competitors jump on their bikes and complete the cycling leg of the race. Finally, after finishing the cycling leg, competitors put on their running shoes and complete the last leg, which is the running leg. Triathlons are a test of endurance, so triathletes need to be well prepared when attempting a triathlon race.

The run is the last leg of a triathlon race.

Equipment

A triathlon combines three different endurance sports. Triathletes need different equipment for each leg of a triathlon race.

Swimming goggles and caps

One of the most important pieces of equipment that a triathlete needs for the swimming leg is a good pair of goggles. Swimming goggles stop eye irritation, allow triathletes to see under water and prevent their vision from being blurred when they lift their heads out of the water. This makes it possible for triathletes to move through a crowd of swimmers and make their way around the swimming course more easily. Triathletes also wear swimming caps, which identify them as competitors in a triathlon race.

Goggles and a swimming cap are worn during the swim leg of a triathlon race.

Running shoes

To complete the run leg of a triathlon race in as fast a time as possible, triathletes need to wear a pair of comfortable, lightweight running shoes. Some triathletes replace the laces in their shoes with elastic laces, which allows them to pull their shoes on and off without having to untie them. This saves valuable time when changing from the cycling leg to the running leg.

A triathlete needs light, comfortable running shoes.

The bike

The cycling leg of a triathlon is always performed on roads, so triathletes use **road-racing bikes**. These lightweight bikes have thin, smooth tyres. This allows triathletes to ride at high speeds. Many triathletes attach **tri-bars** to their handlebars. This allows them to sit in a **streamlined position** with their weight forward. Sitting in this position means that triathletes are able to travel at faster speeds, because the amount of wind resistance is reduced.

Did you know?

Bikes used by elite triathletes can weigh as little as 4 kilograms (8.8 pounds). These bikes are made of strong, lightweight materials, such as carbon fibre.

By using tri-bars, triathletes can lean forward and sit in a streamlined position.

Bike helmet

Triathlon bikes travel at high speeds and accidents can occur, so it is important for triathletes to protect their heads with strong helmets that fit well.

Water bottle

Triathlons can be long and tiring, so it is important for triathletes to drink a lot of fluid during the race. Triathletes need to carry a water bottle on their bikes, and drink from it frequently during the cycling leg.

Cycling shoes

Experienced triathletes wear special cycling shoes that clip into the bike's pedals. This allows a triathlete to generate more power and speed when pedalling.

Clothing

Triathletes need to wear multi-purpose clothing that they can swim, cycle and run in.

Swimming costumes and tank tops

Male triathletes have traditionally worn swimming costumes and **lycra** tank tops. Female triathletes have traditionally worn one-piece swimming costumes. These outfits are lightweight and skin-tight. This means that they are perfect for swimming and running in. However, they are not the most comfortable outfits to cycle in.

Tri-suits

Recently, both male and female triathletes have started wearing one-piece **tri-suits**. These suits are also made of lycra, and are skin-tight and lightweight. They cover a triathlete's thighs, so they are comfortable to cycle in, as well as to swim and run in.

The tri-suit is now the most popular racing outfit for both male and female triathletes.

Wetsuits

Triathletes can wear rubber wetsuits to stay warm when swimming in cold water. These wetsuits can have full-length arms and legs, or full-length legs with a singlet top. Triathletes wear their wetsuits over the top of their lycra tri-suits, so that when they take their wetsuits off after completing the swim leg, they can cycle and run in comfort. Some triathletes cover their legs and arms in baby oil so that they can slip off their wetsuits quickly and easily after the swim leg.

Wetsuits keep triathletes warm if the swimming leg is held in cold water.

The course

A triathlon course is made up of a swimming course, a cycling course, a running course and a **transition area**. In a race, triathletes complete the three courses in order, and use the transition area to change their equipment and clothing in between the different legs.

A triathlon course

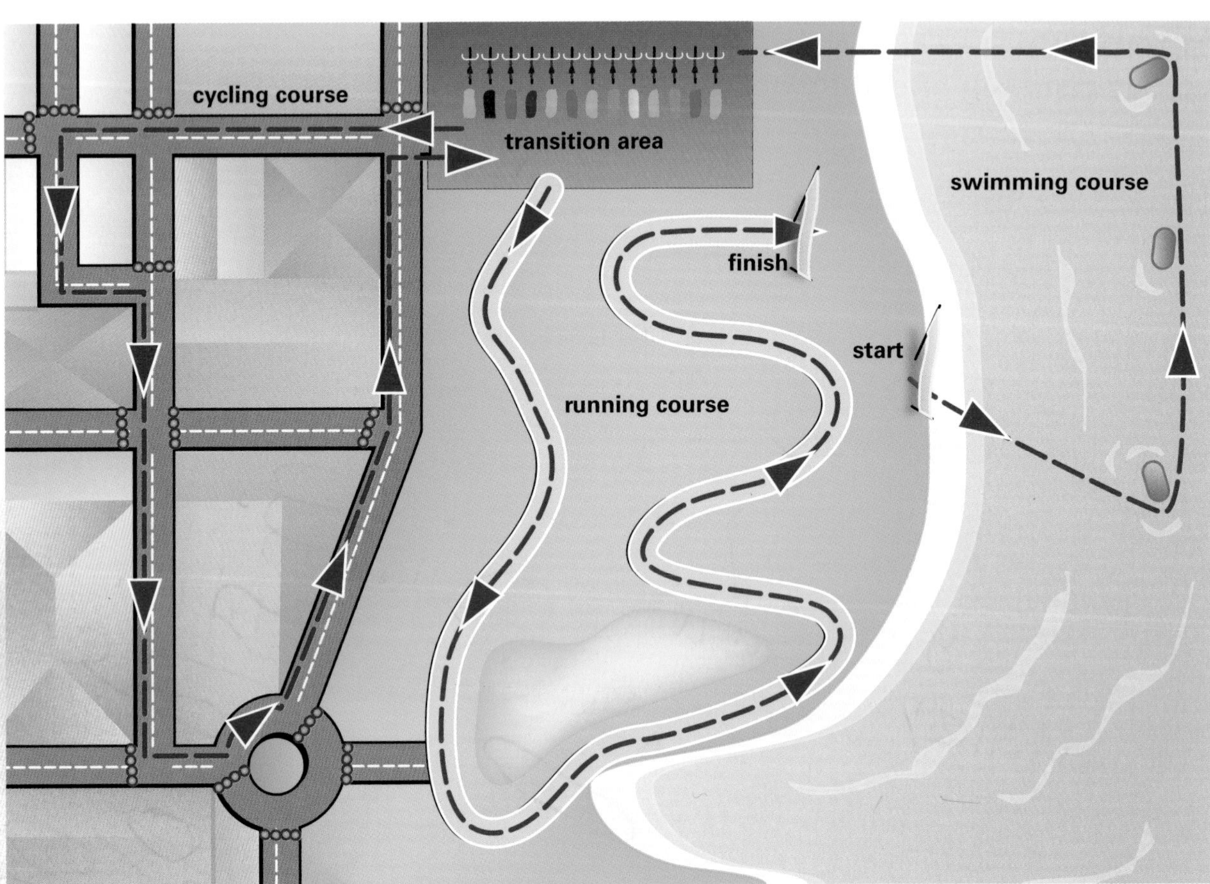

The swimming course

The triathlon swimming course is usually in an ocean beach, a bay, a lake or even a pool. The course is usually marked out by floating marker **buoys**, which the triathletes have to swim around.

The cycling course

The triathlon cycling course is on roads that are close to the swimming course. These roads are always closed to other traffic, so that triathletes do not have to worry about cars. The course is usually marked out by **witches' hats** and signs.

The running course

The triathlon running course is usually on a road or footpath. This course is also marked by witches' hats and signs, and is close to the cycling and swimming courses. The running leg is the final leg of a triathlon, so the run ends at the finish line.

The transition area

The transition area is the place where triathletes can store and change their gear. The three legs of the triathlon require different equipment. Triathletes need a place to change their equipment in between the different legs. Each triathlete is given a bike rack and patch of ground to store their equipment. Triathletes enter the transition area after completing the swim to change gear before beginning the cycling leg. At the end of the cycling leg, they enter the transition area again to leave the bike and begin the running leg.

The transition area is the place where triathletes change their gear and store their equipment.

Did you know?

The running course of the famous Hawaiian Ironman triathlon race is the same length as an Olympic marathon, which is 42 kilometres.

Triathletes

Triathletes come in all shapes and sizes, however, training and competing gives all triathletes a common set of characteristics.

Aerobic fitness

Aerobic fitness means having a well-developed heart and set of lungs that can quickly take in oxygen and move it to the muscles to make energy. Competing in triathlons helps triathletes develop a strong heart and efficient lungs.

Triathlon racing can help people get fit and healthy.

Body fat

Our bodies consist mostly of bone, muscle, water and body fat. Training for triathlons burns a lot of energy and most triathletes burn up some of their body-fat stores. Triathletes usually have low body fat levels.

Muscle fitness

One of the benefits of competing in triathlons is that triathletes develop muscle fitness throughout the whole body. Swimming mainly uses the upper body and legs. Swimming training allows triathletes to develop and tone their chest, shoulder and back muscles, as well as their legs.

Cycling and running mainly use the leg muscles. Cycling training develops the hip, thigh and calf muscles, while running tones all the muscles in the legs and arms. By training and competing in triathlons, triathletes use almost all of the muscles in their bodies. The result is all-round muscle fitness and body tone.

Running training helps to build up the leg muscles.

Swimming skills

The swim is the first leg of a triathlon. To be able to swim the course as quickly and easily as possible, the triathlete needs to master the following skills.

Freestyle swimming stroke

The freestyle swimming stroke is the simplest and fastest competitive swimming stroke, and is the best stroke for triathletes. Most triathletes kick lightly while swimming freestyle. To perform the freestyle stroke, the triathlete follows these steps.

The freestyle stroke

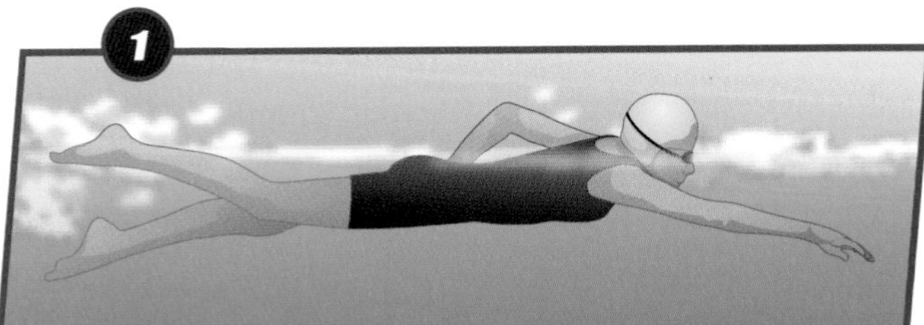

1 The stroke begins with the left hand by the triathlete's side and the right stretched out in front.

2 While pulling backwards through the water with the right arm, the triathlete brings the left arm out of the water and bends the elbow.

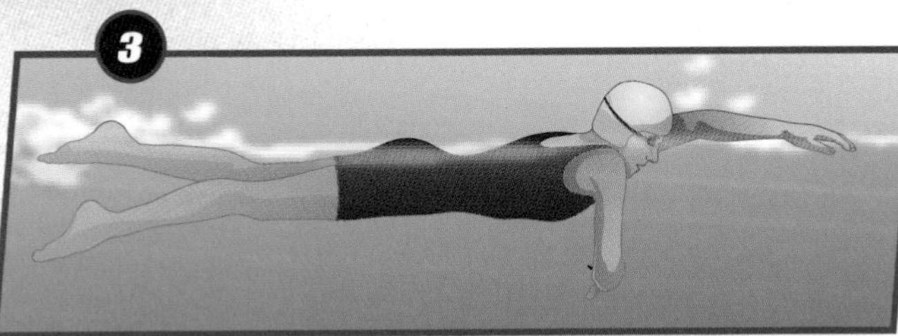

3 The triathlete pulls the right arm under the chest, and pushes it towards the hips while bringing the left arm forward.

4 As the right arm reaches the hip, the triathlete spears the left arm into the water. As the left arm pulls down and the right arm comes out of the water, the triathlete turns the head to the right for a quick breath. Putting the face back into the water, the triathlete slowly breathes out and continues to stroke.

Staying on course

When swimming, triathletes' heads are under water for most of the time. This makes it hard for triathletes to know which direction they are swimming in. To stay on course, triathletes need to pop their heads up out of the water every few strokes to look for the marker buoys. Triathletes take a big stroke and pull down so that the upper body comes out of the water.

By popping their heads out of the water, triathletes can make sure they are swimming in the right direction.

Passing

The swimming course of a triathlon race can be quite crowded. This means triathletes may have to swim around and pass other competitors. When passing, triathletes need to make sure that they do not make contact with other swimmers. By giving each other plenty of room, the swimming course becomes a safer place for all competitors.

Rule

Triathletes are not allowed to use stationary objects, such as a piers or boats, to propel themselves in the water during the swim leg. This is considered unfair forward movement and results in a time penalty.

Cycling skills

The cycling leg of a triathlon race is always the longest leg of the event. It is important for the triathlete to master the following cycling skills to maintain speed throughout this leg.

The upright position gives a triathlete greater control over the bike's movements.

Upright position

The upright position is the most basic riding position. The upright position is used for riding around corners and braking. It involves sitting on the seat with the arms straight and the hands resting on the outer edges of the handlebars. By sitting in this position, triathletes have the greatest control over the bike's steering, gears and brakes.

The streamlined position allows a triathlete to ride at the fastest speed possible.

Streamlined position

The streamlined cycling position is used when a triathlete is riding on a long, straight section of the course. To sit in a streamlined position, the rider leans forward and rests the forearms and hands on the tri-bars. The tri-bars sit in the middle of the handlebars and extend forward. By sitting in this position, the rider can cut through the wind and ride at a faster pace.

Uphill technique

Riding uphill is the most tiring part of the cycling leg of a triathlon race. To be able to ride uphill quickly, triathletes need to be fit and have good uphill technique. When riding up a steep hill, the rider may need to rise off the seat and lean forward over the handlebars. This riding position allows the rider to push down hard on the pedals while riding up the hill.

When riding uphill, triathletes use their bodyweight to push down on the pedals.

Passing

Throughout the cycling leg of a triathlon, triathletes need to pass slower competitors. They need to avoid making contact with other competitors. Before making a move, the triathlete quickly looks around to see if any other riders are coming past or are sitting nearby. If the coast is clear, the triathlete moves out and **accelerates** past the competitor in front.

Rule

During the cycling leg of some triathlons, triathletes are not allowed to use a technique called drafting. Drafting is riding behind another rider so that their bike blocks the wind, which allows the cyclist at the back to go faster. Triathletes need to stay 7 metres (23 feet) from the next rider, unless attempting to pass.

Running skills

The run is the final leg in a triathlon race and is usually where the race is won or lost. Running is a basic skill, but to be able to complete the run in as fast a time as possible, the triathlete needs to use the following skills and tactics.

The running action

To maintain a good pace for long distances, triathletes need a strong and efficient running action. When running, the triathlete:

- keeps the hips and chest high and leans slightly forward
- keeps the shoulders relaxed and moves the arms back and forward with the elbows bent to make an L shape
- keeps the head still and tries to keep the jaw relaxed
- tries to raise the knees high and take long strides
- keeps the leg and arm action straight forward and back, and never across the body.

The running action

Pacing

Pacing means running at a constant speed. The running course of a triathlon is usually quite long, so triathletes need to pace themselves to cover the distance without tiring out too early. For a triathlon race, triathletes aim to run at 70 per cent of their maximum speed. After the cycling leg, the triathlete's legs will feel heavy and tired. The triathlete begins the run leg slowly, but quickly builds up to a normal running pace.

During the run leg of a triathlon, triathletes need to stay relaxed so that they do not lose too much energy.

Passing

During the run leg, triathletes may want to pass or overtake a competitor. To pass successfully, the triathlete needs to run at a faster pace from a few metres behind the competitor. When drawing level with the competitor, the triathlete runs faster again and maintains this speed until safely out in front. The triathlete then returns to normal speed and continues running.

Transitions

To make **transitions** between the different legs in a triathlon race as smooth and as fast as possible, the triathlete needs to use the following tactics.

Equipment layout

Half an hour before the race is due to start, triathletes find their positions in the transition area. These are marked according to the triathlete's race number. Triathletes need to position their equipment in an orderly fashion. The bike is placed on the bike rack with the handlebars curled around the top bar of the rack. Below the bike, the triathlete can place a towel on the ground. The towel is used to wipe mud or sand off the feet after the swim leg, and to stop stones or sand sticking to the bottom of the feet as the triathlete changes shoes after the cycle leg. On top of the towel, the triathlete places the running shoes, cycling shoes (if worn) and helmet. This allows the triathlete to find and use the equipment as quickly as possible. The triathlete can also place this equipment in a crate.

These triathletes have laid out their equipment in an organised way.

The first transition – swim to cycle

After finishing the swim leg of a triathlon race, the triathlete goes to the transition area. On reaching their spot in the transition area, the triathlete takes off the goggles, swimming cap and wetsuit if wearing one. Next, the triathlete puts on the bike helmet and shoes, grabs the bike and wheels it out of the transition area. After leaving the transition area, the triathlete can jump on the bike and ride off.

Rule

A triathlete who mounts the bike before putting on and fastening the helmet receives a time penalty.

Triathletes need to make the cycle-to-run transition as quickly as possible.

The second transition – cycle to run

After completing the cycling leg of the race, the triathlete goes to the transition area again, dismounting the bike before entering the transition station. At the transition station, the triathlete hangs the bike up on the rack, takes off the helmet and changes shoes if wearing different running shoes. After quickly stretching the thighs, the triathlete runs from the transition area to begin the running leg.

Rules and safety

There are a number of general rules that apply to the triathlon race as a whole, as well as specific rules that apply to each leg of the triathlon.

All competing triathletes need to display their race number.

General rules

There are some general rules that triathlon competitors need to follow. Competitors:

- wear a race number during the race, which is given out when they enter
- cannot interfere with another competitor
- follow the course marked out by the marker buoys and witches' hats
- follow the directions of the race officials.

Swimming rules

Some of the rules that apply to the swimming leg of a triathlon are:

- all competitors need to follow the course marked out by the floating marker buoys
- no flippers, paddles or **flotation devices** are allowed
- all competitors need to wear an official swimming cap.

Rule

A triathlete who cannot complete the swim leg needs to raise one arm overhead and pump it up and down. Race officials will then help the competitor out of the water.

Cycling rules

Some of the rules that apply to the cycling leg of a triathlon are:

- all competitors need to wear an approved helmet during the cycling leg
- helmet straps need to be done up at any time the bike is moving
- competitors need to wear a top and shoes during the cycling leg
- competitors are not allowed to ride their bikes through the transition area
- competitors need to follow the course marked out by witches' hats and signs.

Running rules

Some of the rules that apply to the running leg of a triathlon are:

- competitors need to wear a top and shoes during the running leg
- competitors need to follow the course marked out by the witches' hats and signs.

Safety tips

To avoid injuring themselves during a triathlon, competitors need to:

- train for a number of weeks before entering a triathlon
- wear sunscreen to avoid sunburn
- drink plenty of water before, during and after the event. This helps competitors avoid **dehydration**. The cycling leg is the best time to drink during the event.

Triathletes need to drink during the race to avoid becoming dehydrated.

Triathlon fitness

Triathlon racing is a physically demanding sport. Triathletes need to be fit, strong and flexible, and have good heart and lung power. To get the most out of competitions, triathletes need to warm up, cool down and develop fitness by training.

Warming up and cooling down

A triathlon warm-up gets triathletes' muscles warm and stretched so that they can train or compete better. A cool-down stretches the muscles out after training or competing. Triathletes are also less likely to be injured after stretching.

Triathletes can help one another to stretch before a training session.

Shoulder stretch

With one hand, the triathlete reaches behind their neck and as far down their back as possible. With the other hand, the triathlete slowly puts pressure on the elbow of the arm that is being stretched. The triathlete holds the shoulder stretch for 30 seconds, then swaps arms.

Quad stretch

The triathlete stands with one leg straight and the other bent and raised behind. With one hand, the triathlete reaches behind and slowly pulls the foot of the bent leg up towards the buttocks. This stretches the quadriceps muscle, or quad, which is the large muscle on the front of the thigh. The triathlete holds the stretch for 30 seconds, then swaps legs.

Leg roll

The triathlete lies on their back with both arms spread wide, one leg straight and one leg bent. Slowly, the triathlete rolls the bent leg across and over the straight leg, keeping the shoulders flat on the ground. The triathlete touches the ground with the bent knee and holds this position for 30 seconds, before repeating the roll to the other side.

Seated hamstring stretch

Sitting with one leg straight and the other leg bent to the side, the triathlete bends forward at the waist and slowly slides both hands down the straight leg as far as possible. This stretches the hamstring of the straight leg, which runs down the back of the thigh and behind the knee. The triathlete holds the stretch for 30 seconds, then swaps legs.

The hamstring stretch can also be performed in a standing position.

Calf stretch

The triathlete stands close to a wall or fence. Resting both hands on the wall or fence, the triathlete places one leg further back than the other. Keeping the heel of the back foot on the ground and bending the front knee, the triathlete slowly bends both arms and leans in toward the wall or fence. The triathlete feels the stretch in the calf muscle of the straight leg. The triathlete holds the stretch for 30 seconds, then swaps legs.

Trunk stretch

The triathlete lies face-down with both hands under the shoulders and both legs straight. The triathlete slowly straightens the arms and arches the back, keeping both thighs flat on the ground so that the trunk is fully stretched. The triathlete holds the stretch for 30 seconds, then lowers the trunk back to the ground.

Triathlon training

To build up to their first triathlon or to regularly compete in triathlons, triathletes need to complete training sessions. This helps triathletes develop their fitness for each triathlon leg.

Swimming training

To make it through the swimming leg of a triathlon, triathletes need to be able to swim the required distance comfortably. Six weeks is the minimum preparation time for any program, and during that six weeks triathletes need to start with easy sessions and gradually build up their speed and distance.

A swimming training program includes three types of sessions:

- slow and easy swims, in which the triathlete aims to swim continuously over a long distance to build up endurance. The triathlete swims freestyle at a comfortable pace and gradually builds up the distance over the six weeks.
- speed swims, in which the triathlete aims to develop speed in order to get off to a good start in a triathlon race and pass other competitors quickly during the swim leg. A speed session involves a number of 'sprints' over a shorter distance.
- time trials, in which the triathlete practises swimming at race pace over the race distance to see whether they have made improvements.

Triathletes sometimes use hand paddles when training to help them improve their freestyle swimming stroke.

Cycling training

Cycling is usually the easiest leg of a triathlon as long as it is not too windy. The key to the cycling leg is to get into a steady pace that can be comfortably kept up for the whole distance. Cycling training is designed to build up the triathlete's endurance by gradually increasing the distance, along with some speed and hill riding to prepare for all sorts of courses.

Running training

The running leg of a triathlon is probably the hardest because it comes at the end when the triathlete is getting tired. To prepare for the running leg, the triathlete needs to practise running at a steady pace that can be maintained for the full distance. Over the six weeks of the training program, the distance is gradually increased. Triathletes also need to include sprint and hill sessions to build up speed.

When doing running training, some triathletes wear a stopwatch so they can time themselves.

Competition

Each year, triathlon competitions are held in countries all over the world. The popularity of these events is growing all the time.

Local competitions

Triathlon clubs and local organisations hold triathlons for people of all ages throughout the summer months. These triathlons cater for beginners as well as for more experienced triathletes. Recently, some triathlon organisations have started to organise triathlons for children and teenagers. These competitions have become extremely popular and the number of competitors is growing every year. The beginner and children's races are usually held over shorter distances, which are more suitable than those in races for more experienced or professional triathletes.

Rule

In a triathlon race, a competitor can only receive assistance from race officials. Family and friends are not allowed to give a competitor anything, such as food or drink, during the race.

Young athletes can compete in children's triathlons.

Race distances

There are three standard race distances for adult triathlons. These are:

- sprint distance – 750-metre swim/20-kilometre cycle/ 5-kilometre run
- official distance – 1.5-kilometre swim/40-kilometre cycle/ 10-kilometre run
- ultra distance – 3.8-kilometre swim/180-kilometre cycle/ 42-kilometre run.

National series

In countries such as Australia and the United States of America, triathlon organisations run a series of national races for professional triathletes. These races are very competitive and use a variety of race distances. These triathlons draw large crowds and are also shown on television.

World Cup

The World Cup is a series of international events. Triathletes from all over the world compete in these races for prize money. There is a series of events for men and a series for women. The pinnacle of these races is the World Championship, which is held in a different country every year. This race is held over the official triathlon distance. The World Championship is a sought-after prize for professional triathletes.

Winning a World Cup triathlon is a proud moment for a triathlete.

Olympic triathlon

Triathlon races have been part of the Olympic Games since the competition in Sydney 2000. Olympic triathletes compete for their country, not just for individual glory or money. The Olympic program has two triathlon races: the men's individual race and the women's individual race.

Olympic triathlon races are held over the official distance and include a 1.5-kilometre swim, a 40-kilometre cycle, and a 10-kilometre run. The winner of the men's race usually completes the course in approximately 1 hour and 40 minutes, and the winner of the women's race usually finishes in approximately 1 hour and 50 minutes. At the end of the race, the top three triathletes are awarded the gold, silver and bronze medals.

The winner of an Olympic Games triathlon competition receives a gold medal.

Did you know?

Elite triathletes maintain an average speed of more than 40 kilometres per hour throughout the cycling leg of an official-distance race.

Glossary

accelerates increases speed

buoys large floating objects used to mark out the swimming course of a triathlon race

dehydration a condition that occurs when an athlete's body uses too much fluid during a race or training

elite the most skilful triathletes who participate in the highest levels of competition

endurance the ability to continue racing for long periods of time

flotation devices objects used to keep a swimmer afloat

lycra an elastic, skin-tight fabric used in triathlon suits

road-racing bikes bikes used by professional cyclists and triathletes; they have thin wheels, a light frame and racing handlebars

streamlined position a position in which the cyclist leans forward to lessen the resistance created by the wind, allowing them to ride faster

transition area the place where triathletes store their gear in between the three legs of a triathlon race

transitions changes from one leg of a triathlon to the next

tri-bars metal bars with padded armrests that extend forward from the handlebars of a triathlon bike, and allow a triathlete to lean forward while riding

tri-suits special one-piece suits that cover the thighs and are comfortable to wear for all legs of a triathlon race

witches' hats fluorescent, cone-shaped markers used to mark out the cycling and running courses for a triathlon

Index